GRIZZLY BEARS
Fierce Hunters

Lucy Sackett Smith

PowerKiDS
press

New York

To Peter "Gramps" Cantono, who gives the best bear hugs in the whole wide world

Published in 2010 by The Rosen Publishing Group, Inc.
29 East 21st Street, New York, NY 10010

First Edition

Editor: Nicole Pristash
Book Design: Kate Laczynski
Photo Researcher: Jessica Gerweck

Photo Credits: Cover, p. 1 Daniel J. Cox/Getty Images; p. 5 © Morales/Age Fotostock; p. 7 © Kennan Ward/Corbis; p. 9 © www.istockphoto.com/Stephen Schwartz; pp. 10–11 © John E. Marriott/Age Fotostock; p. 13 Michael S. Quinton/Getty Images; p. 15 © Paul A. Souders/Corbis; p. 17 © Daniel J. Cox/Corbis; p. 19 © Joe McDonald/Corbis; p. 21 Paul Oomen/Getty Images.

Library of Congress Cataloging-in-Publication Data

Smith, Lucy Sackett.
  Grizzly bears : fierce hunters / Lucy Sackett Smith. — 1st ed.
    p. cm. — (Mighty mammals)
  Includes index.
  ISBN 978-1-4042-8106-6 (lib. bdg.) — ISBN 978-1-4358-3283-1 (pbk.) —
ISBN 978-1-4358-3284-8 (6-pack)
  1. Grizzly bear—Juvenile literature. I. Title.
  QL737.C27S616 2010
  599.784—dc22
                              2009002737

Manufactured in the United States of America

CONTENTS

What Are Grizzly Bears?

Grizzly bears are among the biggest, strongest, and most-feared animals in the United States and Canada. However, these big bears also **inspire** people. Grizzlies help people understand the beauty and power of wild nature.

Grizzly bears are a kind of brown bear. A brown bear is a **species** of bear that lives in Asia, Europe, and North America. People use the name "grizzly bear" when talking about brown bears that live inland in North America. Grizzly bears get their name because their coats become grizzled, or tipped with gray, as they get older.

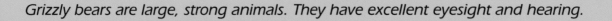

Grizzly bears are large, strong animals. They have excellent eyesight and hearing.

North American Bears

Most grizzly bears live in the inland parts of Alaska and western Canada. However, there are also between 1,000 and 1,500 grizzly bears in the Rocky Mountains in Wyoming, Washington, Montana, and Idaho. Many of these southern grizzly bears live in parks, such as Yellowstone National Park and North Cascades National Park.

Many grizzly bears live in grassy fields on mountains. Other grizzlies can be found in the woods. In northern Alaska and Canada, some grizzly bears live on tundras. Tundras are cold, dry plains with almost no trees where some of the ground is frozen all year.

A tundra, shown here, may look empty, but it has a lot of plants and berries for grizzly bears to eat.

How to Spot a Grizzly Bear

Grizzly bears are powerful animals. These large bears generally weigh between 200 and 800 pounds (91–363 kg)! Grizzlies have fat under their skin and thick fur to keep them warm. They also have long, **curved** claws.

As all brown bears do, grizzlies have bumps over their shoulders. This is one way you can tell grizzlies apart from black bears. These two bear species often live in the same places. It is harder to tell grizzlies apart from Alaskan coastal brown bears or Kodiak bears. However, these other kinds of North American brown bears tend to be even larger than grizzlies.

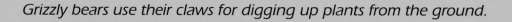
Grizzly bears use their claws for digging up plants from the ground.

MIGHTY FACTS

1. Even though grizzlies are kinds of brown bears, their coats can be black, cream, or cinnamon colored, as well as brown.

2. Brown bears, including grizzlies, have smaller, rounder ears than black bears have.

3. The foreheads and noses of grizzlies and other brown bears curve in, unlike those of black bears.

4. Grizzlies sometimes stand up on their back legs to take a look around.

5. From time to time, a grizzly will use an old den for its winter sleep. However, grizzlies generally build new dens each year.

6 A grizzly's **sense** of smell and hearing are excellent. The bear's sense of sight is about as good as a person's is.

7 Female grizzly bears start having babies when they are about five or six years old. This is quite old for an animal.

8 Grizzly bears generally live between 20 and 30 years in the wild.

A Bear's Life

Grizzly bears are generally solitary. This means that they spend most of their time on their own, rather than with other bears. Grizzly bears share their **home ranges** with other grizzlies, but the bears tend to stay away from each other. Grizzly ranges may be several hundred square miles (sq km) large. The bears need lots of room to look for food.

Grizzly bears generally look for food in the morning and the evening. Grizzlies are **omnivores**. This means that they eat both plants and meat. Grizzlies often remember good places to find food from earlier years, and they come back to these same spots.

When young grizzly bears are not looking for food, they often rest and play!

The Sleepy Season

As fall comes, grizzlies eat more and more food to get ready for the coming winter. A grizzly's body turns the food it eats into fat. The fat will supply the animal with **energy** throughout the cold winter, when food is very hard to find.

Grizzly bears also save energy by sleeping through the winter in their dens. Bears generally dig dens before the cold weather sets in. Grizzlies line the dens with bedding, such as evergreen branches and dead leaves and grass. Then, the bears curl up in it and fall asleep. Grizzly bears do not even eat or drink during their deep winter sleep.

During the part of the year when grizzlies are not resting in a winter sleep, they often take naps during the day.

Grizzly Cubs

During the winter sleep, grizzly bear mothers do not wake up at all, even when they are giving birth to their babies! Mother grizzlies generally have two babies at a time. Grizzly cubs, as the babies are known, are born in January or February. Newborn cubs have no hair, and they weigh less than 1 pound (.5 kg). The tiny cubs drink their mothers' milk, and they grow quickly. The little cubs sleep a lot, but they do not sleep as deeply as their mothers do.

When spring comes, mother grizzly bears wake up. They leave their dens with their cubs and search for food.

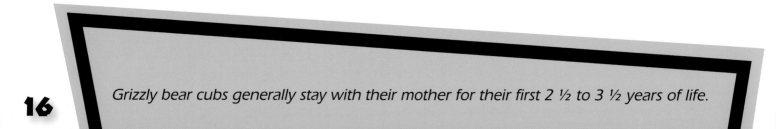

Grizzly bear cubs generally stay with their mother for their first 2 ½ to 3 ½ years of life.

I'll Eat Anything!

Grizzly bears eat dozens of kinds of plants. In the spring, the bears eat flowers, such as dandelions and clovers. Berries are a good meal for them in the fall. Grizzlies also eat many grasses, nuts, **roots**, and **mushrooms**.

Though grizzly bears eat mostly plants, they do eat some meat. Grizzlies are very powerful hunters. They use their long claws to dig up **rodents** from the rodents' underground homes. The bears also eat insects, such as ants, moths, and grubs. Grizzlies catch fish, and they even eat dead animals! In the spring, they hunt young moose, deer, and **caribou**.

When getting ready for their winter sleep, grizzly bears may eat up to 90 pounds (41 kg) of food each day.

Staying Safe Around Grizzlies

Though they do not generally hunt people, grizzly bears can be very **dangerous**. Grizzlies are huge, powerful animals that can badly hurt, or even kill, a person. Grizzlies are fast. They can run as fast as 30 miles per hour (48 km/h)!

Bears are extra dangerous when they are **protecting** their cubs. Never go near a grizzly that is with its cubs. Grizzly bears will also **attack** people who come near their food supplies. Never move toward a bear. However, if a bear comes up to you, do not run away. Stand still, wave your arms slowly, and talk firmly to the bear.

Grizzly bears try to stay away from people. They generally attack humans only when they are protecting themselves or their cubs.

Wild and Wonderful

Grizzly bears are the top animals in the places they live. These bears are so big that **predators** almost never attack adult grizzlies. Wild cats called cougars sometimes attack cubs. However, mother bears often drive cougars away.

People are the grizzly bear's main predator. People hunt grizzlies and take over their land. Grizzly bears once lived throughout the American West, but they have been almost wiped out there. Happily, there are still lots of grizzlies in Alaska. Grizzlies are making a comeback in national parks, too, thanks to the hard work of many people. These big, wild bears are here to stay!

GLOSSARY

attack (uh-TAK) To try to hurt someone or something.

caribou (KER-eh-boo) Large deer that live in the North American Arctic.

curved (KURVD) Having a shape that bends or curls.

dangerous (DAYN-jeh-rus) Might cause hurt.

energy (EH-nur-jee) The power to work or to act.

home ranges (HOHM RAYNJ-ez) Places in which an animal generally stays.

inspire (in-SPY-ur) To fill with interest and strong feeling.

mushrooms (MUSH-roomz) Small, plantlike living things that are often shaped like umbrellas. Many mushrooms can be eaten, but some can cause harm.

omnivores (OM-nih-vorz) Animals that eat both plants and animals.

predators (PREH-duh-terz) Animals that kill other animals for food.

protecting (pruh-TEK-ting) Keeping safe.

rodents (ROH-dents) Animals with gnawing teeth, such as mice.

roots (ROOTS) The parts of plants or trees that are underground.

sense (SENS) One of the powers an animal uses to learn what is around it, such as hearing and sight.

species (SPEE-sheez) One kind of living thing. All people are one species.

INDEX

WEB SITES

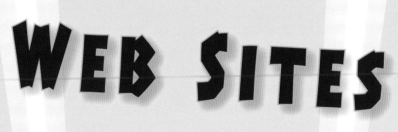

Due to the changing nature of Internet links, PowerKids Press has developed an online list of Web sites related to the subject of this book. This site is updated regularly. Please use this link to access the list:
www.powerkidslinks.com/mamm/bear/